Reflections of a Forbidden Love

Nicole Enna

BookLeaf Publishing

India | USA | UK

Presentation by *BookLeaf Publishing*

Web: www.bookleafpub.com

E-mail: info@bookleafpub.com

ISBN: 9789358310375

First edition 2023

ACKNOWLEDGEMENT

First and foremost a huge thank you to the Lord up above for speaking directly to me, allowing me to be open, bestow honest wisdom, while holding nothing back. In addition to everyone who has touched my heart and soul making my feelings transition into written words with pen and paper. I appreciate all of the inspiring material in helping me to achieve this valuable treasure.

PREFACE

In this book each poem tells its own story which includes the evolution of love found, love lost and love re-awakened. It is based on overwhelming feelings of love, happiness, joy, sorrow and heartbreak, some which were built up over time. It truly is without a shadow of doubt, divine intervention with a roller coaster of emotions expelled from the heart. Each relationship is your own genuine experience, a learning process, a chance to find yourself, what you are willing to accept and decide if it truly is what you want for your life. Be grateful for all of the roads winding twists and turns, along this path is where you are supposed to be. Use your intuition and let fate guide you in discovering your own remarkable destiny.

ADDICTION

-He's the one addiction I knowingly possess,
should have overdosed years ago I've loved him
in excess
-In my blood, throughout my brain, his heart
intravenously runs through my veins
-A seven year prescription, no known expiration
date, one too many refills..forgiving a smeared
slate
-I've put up with your side effects which may
have caused me pain, guess we'll never know
why I cant abstain
-Snap your fingers, pinch me..do what you must
do..how do I wean off of the one & only you?
-Shaking sick & nauseated, withdrawals like
sweat & tears..I'll love you forever yet kick this
addiction conquering all of my fears

FANTASY

-Sitting here dazed, mesmerized by this preview,
got me feeling things I never thought I'd feel for
you
-Make me bite my lip, got me lookin' away,
feeling crazy inside just wanna have my way
-Probably one of the sexiest auras I've ever met
& living in my fantasy world, the dates already
been set
-Take me away into your bliss, pull me in closer
with a long, passionate kiss
-Gotta get it outta my system, maybe get a room
at the Wyndham, simply cuz I can't resist him
-Eyes deeper than the oceans' floor, smile sexier
than a lions' roar
-Don't know how much longer I can stay
contained, these feelings I'm having can't be
restrained
-The attraction's magnetic, intense, pulsating
waves..shaking my head cuz I gotta behave
-Doubt you've ever contemplated these same
exact thoughts, but I wanna be the queen to your
fine king of hearts
-Feeling pathetic for feeling this way, wish I
were able to call you my bae

-Never thought I'd get free from outta his rivets,
so if anything thanks for lifting my spirits
-You're amazing & awesome rolled all in one &
wow, just like that, this fantasy's done!
The balls in your court, I just thought you should
know, if you're down, I'm down, it'll stay on the
low

MMMN MMMN MMMN

-Let me tell you about my Italian dream, no, not
meatballs & spaghetti..close ya eyes, relax,
inhale..exhale..slow & steady
-Flashes of the night piece together a story, but
to tell it I must sip some Campari
-Bitter & spicy with sweet complex notes, while,
offering assets too suggestive to quote
-The "how bout some D___" line, it's all in good
fun, the obvious flirting still getting work done
-Like an onion his layers are deep..sexy,
charming, funny & sweet
-Attraction like I can't explain, it's more than I
could ever sustain
-Body made into a machine, praying God will
intervene
-Some say he's a well done like type of steak,
but baby skip the ketchup, just slide into this
lake
-He's one of a kind, med rare at the core, every
time I see him my heart drops to the floor
-If he's the espresso in my tasty latte, MMMN,
MMMN, MMMN, let me sip it all day
-The sexiness steadily oozes on out, the fish of
the year, he's my speckled trout

-My tiramisu with whip cream on top "a lil slice
of heaven" this boy better stop!
-His life is a mess & well, yea mine is too,
simply more proof why I should never pursue
-A work in progress at the construction site,
checks out, it's good, you got the green light
-Clearly I must be smoking on dope, but what if
there were a glimmer of hope? Ha! Lol, real talk
tho, nope!
-Can't seem to get my eye off of the prize,
ironically hoping he's equally wise
-MMMN MMMN MMMN I'll say it again, just
let me know how, which way & when..

NAKED HEART

-My naked heart craves you, every breath of air
is a gift
-Although its new, fresh & exciting, those eyes
& smile are enticingly inviting
-I don't know what's next to come..& damn,
really..where'd you come from?
-The adventures of you keep me intrigued,
you're all that I want & soulfully need
-I challenge you to accept my love & will treat
you with dignity & respect thereof
-I welcome the thought of making memories
with you, even if we never got to go to the zoo
-I only wanna keep a smile on ya face,
mystifying, enamored, embrace this sexy space
-Thanks for making me the happiest I've been in
a very long time & if you didn't already know,
well baby you're a dime
-Never want this feeling to end, my naked heart
seeks yours & my puzzle piece transcends

PRICELESS GIFT

-Would you think it was rude if I came off so
blunt, can see us together I can't even front
-Let me be the princess better yet the queen,
come swoop me away in a black, stretched out
limousine
-Don't worry about the attire, it's you I'm tryina'
admire
-Smiles the length of a basketball court, but
these walls built up strong as a medieval fort
-Hangin' outta the open sunroof, lost in his eyes
seeing the proof
-Strands of hair blowing, conversation steady
flowing
-Blows me away with his oversized brain,
holding on tight, boutta switch outta this lane
-Zoom..traveling further into outer space,
smokin' a J in this red sexy lace
-Sip idty sip sip on this pink moscato, sing to me
in falsetto with notes of vibrato
-Wrap me up tight, don't let this night go, kissin'
my lips like a specialized pro
-Reaching the steepest climax with this priceless
gift, feeling intense vibrations as the continents
slowly drift

-Runnin' away with my imagination what more can I say, just wanted to wish you the happiest of birthdays bae

REFLECTIONS OF A FORBIDDEN LOVE

-Like the apple itself his love is forbidden, but
it's so hard to keep all of my feeling hidden
-I knew in my heart that we could never be, but
that didn't stop him from pursuing me
-I thought it'd be cool to hangout & chill but
he's on top of his game & the brotha's got skill
-I blew it off like it was no big deal, but never in
wildest dreams could I imagine the happiness
that I'd feel
-My feelings grew stronger as I was colorblind
to race, I'll forever cherish his soft kisses &
warm bear hug embrace
-Though it was never meant to go this far, I've
escaped to paradise on a shooting star
-Flying high as a kite but how long can this last,
a blank staring gaze knows it's almost the past
-Riding up & down on this roller coaster, what
stop button to press, how did I get caught up in
this emotional mess?
-Crashing waves under a cloud of rain, drenched
I am soaking in pain
-As tears put out a candles' burning fire, my
heart still bleeds with a passionate desire

-Though he can never be mine to call my own,
he was awesome to borrow, thanks for the loan
-I have to say thank you for touching my soul,
I'm eternally grateful & spiritually whole
-As two caterpillars shed their cocoon, one day
we'll be butterflies, can the next lifetime be
soon?

SMITTEN

-In the stars it's already been written, with his eyes & smile, I've become SMITTEN
-As I drift off in thought, biting my lip, just reminiscing made my heart skip
-Feels so good being in your arms, I think I've found my good luck charm
-Scooped it up, put it in my pocket, now throw away the key & lock it
-It makes me happy being in his presence, his aura reflects that of fluorescence
-Warm, humble, sweet, no one else can compete
 Sexy as hell that look, touch & smell
-Floating high on cloud nine, our bodies gently intertwine
-Feels too good to really be true, gotta give it to God with an eagle eye view
-He's my fairy tale I'm willing to bet, put it all on 36 black, spin that roulette
-He sets the bar high & can not be outdone, SMITTEN I am & have been from day one
-Hopefully he feels what I'm feeling back..if not this whole SMITTEN thing is whack

STOLEN TIME

-This pandemic hit the world with fear, life
beyond today is seemingly unclear
-Am I living in the twilight zone, this virus got
us socially alone
-Distance from my money doesn't pay the bills,
gotta crawl before you walk these are mountains
not just hills
-This must be the Apocalypse, it's like I've lived
these words before straight from Tupac's lips
-Whats going on in the world today, we need to
come together & pray
-All we have are ourselves in the end, these are
different times now, survival my friend
-Glad I experienced a once innocent life, the
80's & 90's, nintendos & bikes
-Kids today will never know, the more you
learn, the more you'll grow
-Nothing but time to ponder away of the ones in
my past who never stray
-How do I stop this contagious spread, with
nothing but memories taking over my head
-I've learned something new from each one yet
still broken, been stuck in this time warp & I'm
not even joking

-Been thinking of someone new quite a lot, but
don't know if there's room to create space on the
spot
-I yearn for something real & raw..passion & fire
fill my hearts one & only desire
-I miss you yes, I miss you so, you're like the
Corona, infectious my beau
-Got me burning up like a fever, succumbing to
his vibes, I'm getting weaker
-For so long my hear'ts been in quarantine, is it
too much to ask to be someone's Queen?
-Acting like it's a victimless crime, an invisible
enemy stealing our time

TIME WILL TELL

-Maybe one day he'll know my love is real &
we'll get to feel all we've waited for for so long
-Maybe he'll know we were made to be together,
soulmates thru every season we've weathered
-Maybe he'd trust this truth if I could show him,
never cheat or lie, don't want us to be broken
-Only time will tell still I know he is the one, I
want us to be happy..our journey's just begun
-Not only is he my best friend but my ride or die
til the very end
-I'm enamored by this special man, wanna spend
our lives walking hand in hand
-My sexy, sweet cinnamon roll, he may not
realize how he's touched my soul
-Talking life & sports all hours of the night, wish
I could hop on a red eye & take the fastest flight
-Wrap my arms around you, kiss your sensual
lips..passion ignites our bodies into a solar
eclipse
-Wiggle my nose, tap my toes, be there in a few,
if only to look deep in your eyes..my baby I love
you

TOO GOOD TO BE TRUE

-Tho it came fast outta nowhere, that pectoral
fin, shame on me for letting you in
-I'm resilient as they come but again this feeling,
my body is numb
-He's playing games its an obvious truth, too bad
his game is dry as vermouth
-Cried my eyes out, it hurts to the core, I now
have to ignore his false lure
-Trying to twist my emotions into multiple
knots, his actions alone show he's steady stirring
the pot
-Guess he feels as if he has all the power, enjoys
getting a rise, ignoring me..every second, minute
& hour
-Pampering & forehead kisses only to be misled,
when he's the one who pursued full speed ahead
-What he's doing just isn't cool, plain & simple,
it's actually cruel
-Little does he know I've gotten his alert..keep
going, don't turn back, leave him in the dirt
-I thought he was different but he showed me his
hand, these destructive winds I can no longer
withstand
-Too bad I thought your intentions were true, too
good to be true, I already knew

TRADED

-Like running back in the NFL, you have just
been cut..traded..in exchange for a first round
draft pick that doesn't belong on the sideline
-A time to shine like a million dollar dime,
undrafted you were found in the rough..not
gonna be easy but gotta stay tough
-Like a defensive back I've got my walls built
up, can't tear it down this D is too strong..can't
bring me down, that will take too long
-Though always in my heart you'll forever
remain..time to trade up & get out of pain
-Endurance is key, gotta stay on that grind, no
doubt forever you'll be on my mind
-New draft picks await, as you no longer love
me it may seem..thanks for the memories we
made as a team
-I didn't see it coming, that blind sighted sack,
you know who you are my special "pin of jack"

LOVE WILL INTERVENE

-Thoughts of you overtake my brain, I can
barely breathe, suffocating in pain
-The wound is deep & talk is cheap, I want the
chance to take that leap
-How I miss you, you'll never know, I want my
baby back with a glass of merlot
-Can't elaborate enough these feelings of
disbelief & even harder to fathom the magnitude
of grief
-Sorry I took you for granted, never wanted to
push you away, I know now that I love you &
need you in my life to stay
-You ground me & keep me on track without
stray, much like the hands who molded our clay
-You make me happy & a better person, I wanna
continue growing & learning
-I'm willing to make the sacrifices necessary for
change, though we're very different, ready to do
whatever it takes to interchange & rearrange
-Will never accept or feel real that it's over, if
anything this break will only bring us closer
-Oh dear Lord, please take the wheel, strengthen
our bond into what's made of steel
-Let down our walls, just let me in, gaining trust
again is where we'll begin

-I want you to be my king and I will be your
queen, Fredrico & Nicolette, love will intervene

SINCERELY

-Hyperventilating can't catch my breath, gasping for air it hurts deep in my chest
-Can't stop crying for hours straight, longing to be in his arms again, he's undoubtedly fate
-This pain is deeper than I could've ever imagined, deep in my heart can still feel his passion
-Aching and yearning to have my baby back, without him isn't right I'm entirely out of whack
-My life is so empty without you on the daily, you think I'm getting myself back at all? Well think again, just barely
-I miss you more than I could ever express, honest to God I'm a hot mess in distress
-I need one more chance to hold you again, the time & place, I'm just asking when?
-Without you in my life time moves extra slow, lonely, sad & lost, tell me where'd you go?
-Waiting for your text or call, days go by & nothing at all
-To hold you, kiss you, look you in your eyes, it's way too early to say our goodbyes
-Unfinished business now that I'm aware, trust me when I say that what we have is rare

-I can feel the flame as I envision our kiss, it's
one of pure bliss that can't be dismissed
-I'm opening up my soul in hopes getting
through, I'm all beat up from head to toe, my
heart is black & blue
-Falling faster into this sinkhole, I simply can
not do this & am truthfully not whole
-My heart is so heavy, life's incomplete, please
come back & sweep me off of my feet
-Giving it to God, he hears me as I pray, yet
steadily reminiscing all hours of the day
-I need you back cuz there's no other you, I love
you baby, sincerely I do

SECOND CHANCE

-Stuck in a gaze of my own living hell, trying to live inside of this vacant shell

-When & where is my happy ending, everything reminds me of you, guess it's break, no bending

-I hate that we really ended up here, devastated looking back in the rear

-So many memories still yet to be made, but out of your life you want me to fade

-It's been so long since I've seen your face, it's like you've disappeared without even a trace

-Can't fight this feeling that we still have a chance, everything about my life you without a doubt enhance

-What can I do to be better for you, communicate what you need me to

-How do I balance the space that you need, it's so hard to fall back as I continue to bleed

-Thoughts of you steadily stacking, I can hear in my head all the jokes that you're cracking

-Unraveling at the seams, I'm quickly coming undone, cuz for me I know you're the only one

-I wanna be the one standing by your side & know that in me you can always confide

-Hold my hand I promise you'll see, there's no denying our chemistry

-Imagine we're at the fair again..we lock eyes at
first glance, let's run it back just one more time,
I need a second chance

A HEARTS' SOLO RAMBLE

-As I meditate in this moment, I see the value of the storm, even while it's quiet, in my mind he still performs
-Been devoured by his show while in this gorgeous gown, that K don't stand for king, yet still he wears his crown
-This susceptible vulnerability isn't any way to live but somehow has a comfort that only he can give
-His delicate, gentle touch is a gift this goddess loves, has gone on for years now, can smell his sweet hugs while my heart strings are strongly tugged
-Think of you more than you ever will know, along with all the wisdom you selflessly bestow
-I've fallen for you after all of these years & now I gotta fall back.. my heart has turned charcoal, a definite carbon black
-Please take me with you on the next step of your journey, bless me with every breath, don't try to deter me
-This chaos within is naked, quite stripped & raw edged emotions can't predict, just depict

-Constant feelings of hurt, guilt & shame as
insecurities mount into one fluid flame
-Pause, think & listen, no need for self
crucifixion
-My soul is full as I hold you in the night, taking
in the beats as our two hearts ignite
-Why must it be so hard to simply go with the
flow, meanwhile never knowing when we'll hit
our final plateau
-To piece back together these fragments from
theft, a hearts' solo ramble is all that is left

ONE GODDESS

-A magnificent vision of beauty melted into
wax, touched by a magnitude of insecurities vast
-Always frantic voice beneath a cloud of fluff,
recall a smearing flood behind a mist of tongue
-Music is a raw whisper, an otherwise nagging
scream, rusting away in my eardrum til your
explosive strong will is done
-Achy winter nights leave delicate summer heat,
eternity is cold, yet manipulative power does not
sweat the smell of the winds' greet
-Cries are embraced, devoured by night entwine
the darkness into the light
-A bleeding puncture wound of an essential
apparatus leak, deprives this gorgeous pink rose
whose thorns appear to be weak
-This lazy repulsive void & bitter drunken skin,
how shallow is a moment grown in the garden of
sin
-One goddess listens carefully & does as she is
told, sweet like the sacred sound of a symphony
for you are the clay of his mold
-One goddess prays for the gift to be heard,
preciously lather in love giving thanks to his
almighty word

HIS PRISONER OF WAR

-What am I doing, what have I done? My sins
are in front of me, there is nowhere to run
-Losing myself along with my pride, he'll never
be mine, she was his bride
-When is too much simply enough? When does
the road stop being rough?
-For so long I believed all the lies that he told,
but I see them so clear now that they're written
in BOLD!
-He'll leave her one day, come back to me so I
thought..but he'll never leave home, once again
that's his heart
-It's abusive & addictive, something must
give..going half crazy, this is no way to live
-Thinking beaucoup thoughts of sweet memories
made over the years..overwhelmed!!! Crying
gravely..floating in 8 feet of tears
-Reminiscing & smirking bout the places we've
"hid," I want him to love me the way he once
did
-With hope, love & patience all in limbo, my
heart refuses to let him go
-I need faith & courage but can't do this
alone..wisely follow his commandments as they
are written in stone

-As I confess my soul to the man up above, why do I feel guilty when he's the one that I love?
-Though I'm caught in the midst of "enemy force winds," inside of the wreckage my heart remains pinned..
-So alone & depressed aching for him, as my life falls deep into a blackhole of grim
-I wanna be loved & cherished once more, instead of living like his prisoner of war

Remember Paradise

-I surrender this sweet vision, as its beauty basks
in a summer of glisten
-A sugary candy rose of magnificence, recalls
delicious warm honeys' innocence
-A strong & dark gleam taste like a smile, while
the flickering fire between head & heart can't
reconcile
-The aroma that this arrow desires, escapes a
cherished touch of each target prior
-The hunger incubated in his squeeze, yet still
left stuck in a paralyzed freeze
-Though this soul may feel soulfully
malnourished, under a rock lies the shadow of
courage
-From the depth of his soul to the tatts on his
sleeve, I grieve as what I got to receive had to
leave
-The best gift anyone ever could send, escaping
in time forever again
-Caressing this fantasy although it wasn't
pretend, remembering paradise til my fragile
heart mends

NATURAL DISASTER

-Natural disaster after disaster my world has
come to an end, it's not the same anymore & I
don't know how to even just be his friend
-Our roots are lifting, leaves falling off the tree,
our relationship decaying, rotting away in me
-How deep does it hurt? Vast as the sea..sky high
pleasure can't turn pain into ecstasy
-What we used to have was a warm sunny day,
but now is somehow overcast in my heart
everyday to stay
-Like packing for a hurricane expecting mass
destruction, it's hard to leave what you treasure
behind but must listen to divine instruction
-Empty as a volcano after its erupted, the lava
like my feelings discarded & rejected
-Without any warning, too late to take heed,
tornadoes blow thru tumbleweeds
-Stuck in the rubble of devastation, our time like
an earthquake shattered & forsaken
-Don't allow yet another tsunami to hit, it's
happen one time too many times & therefore I
quit
-While my love for him will reside in endless
craters on the moon, flowing tears rise in flood
waters of this bleeding open wound

-Her name in itself is a Natural Disaster..good
luck weathering the cold nasty "Breeze,"
thought you might rot in hell but now I'm
certain you'll freeze!

UNFOLDS AS IT SHOULD

-Comparing apples to oranges like pears to grapes, why is it so hard to figure out my fate?
-My heart feels one thing while mind says another..Cocoa Krispies or Lucky Charms..hmmn, I want my four leaf clover
-Time & history invested in one while new current events try to reign, still my past is not done
-Rehashing open wounds of "what if he was gone?" How would I live this new found life, how could I move on?
-His love is like a twister..has got my heart in a spin..I tried so hard & fought for the prize that I would win
-So what would really happen if I let him go, so caught up in the moment..he drifts back into my mind like snow
-I guess this contemplation is harder then I thought, how impossible to choose what's predestined from the start
-I should take a leap of faith & know I'll finish strong..pigs will fly forever & I'll stay on top like King Kong
-Runnin' back & forth as if I'm in a race, caterpillar to butterfly, I'm done with just in case

-Fire & water like earth to air, please tell me a
secret..whose soul should I bare?
-A precious flying unicorn or purple people
eater..the answer is in your hands now, for the
universe sweeter!!

WOOL OVER MY EYES

-Always trust your gut, you knew he was a
snake, only time would reveal he's nothing but a
fake
-Every word he utters clearly is a lie, don't know
why I stuck around, I could see through him
clear as the sky
-Tried to open my heart and give him a honest
chance, til I was bored to death with the
ramblings of his stance
-Who the F really cares about political social
media, only to reiterate like a vomiting
encyclopedia
-Shaking my head at how disgusting you are,
why would I even have traveled that far?
-Wonders who he thinks he is, a lawyer to be?
Ha! You can't even defend me
-A selfish lil bitch only bowing to himself,
nothing but a pauper bragging of his wealth
-Contemplating why you're so lonely and sad,
WOW! Take a step back, look at the amazing
girl you once had
-Never will you pull the wool over my eyes, you
thought I was different? Yea, F you,
Surpriiiiiise!

9 789358 310375